# The CA$H RESIDENCE
# for **FAMILIES**

## David A. Saucer

David A. Saucer

# Critical Praise for *The CA$H Residence*

"In *The CA$H Residence*, author David Saucer crystallizes the complex and makes it incredibly simple. He dishes out an understanding of PES (Personalized Economic System) like a gourmet chef serves a fine meal; only Saucer gives you the whole satisfying taste in what seems like one savory bite...Saucer makes the American Dream seem doable and achievable even on a limited household income. He removes the confusion and the sense of overwhelming and replaces it with financial hope. Consistency, long-term commitment, and a simple strategy equate to a debt free and prosperous life with you in the driver's seat...As one who has purchased countless books that cost me money but never provided a return on my investment, I delight in discovering this goldmine in print that opens an immediate pathway to lifetime financial freedom."

Dr. Fred Childs, Executive Coach, Mentor,     Author, Entrepreneur, and Minister

"In my opinion, the book you currently hold in your hand is one of the most concise and relevant in the market today... David Saucer has over two decades of experience in the financial services industry. His ability to communicate intricate financial ideas in a simple manner will make this book a very valuable resource."

> B. Chase Chandler, Best-Selling Author of *The Wealthy Physician* and *The Wealthy Family*

"I have read David's book cover to cover, and I believe that it will help anyone who is looking to be more efficient with their dollars. Creating long term wealth is not about a particular investment vehicle, but about process. David does a great job of explaining the process of how we should all think about our money, and also explains the instrument that can be used to warehouse the dollars until a great opportunity presents itself."

> Jay Gentry (Financial Services Industry Veteran)

"It was not until I watched a family member's 401k take serious losses during 2008 that I began to consider retirement options. I'm not a big fan of losing money that I worked hard for. Neither am I fond of worrying over uncontrollable risks, fees, and uncertain future tax rates. After some personal research and a conversation with David, I realized there was another way to gain my projected goal for retirement as well as have access to my money if I needed it punishment free."

> Reverend Michael Nutter

"David has taken the complex and made it accessible! This book is carefully crafted and filled with meaningful examples. A user-friendly read."

> Dr. Robert Hogan, Assistant Professor of Accounting

☐

"The CA$H Residence is more than a book about how to best invest your money; there are lots of books that do that. But this is a book that will change the way you think about investing. It challenges the conventional wisdom using simple, straight-forward language, not complicated financial jargon. It makes its case plain using Biblical principles and real-world analogies. This book made me completely change the way I plan my retirement. Thank you, David, for your insights!"

> Chuck Drvol, Valued Client

# The CA$H Residence

The Cash Residence for Families
Copyright © 2015 by (David Saucer)

Printed in USA

David A. Saucer

*To my girl, Cindy, and our children, Kaleb and Chloe'*
*Thank you for following me when I chose a less-traveled path.*

**Two roads diverged in a wood, and I —**
**I took the one less traveled by,**
**and that has made all the difference.**
**~ Robert Frost**

David A. Saucer

# **TABLE OF CONTENTS**

# Forward by B. Chase Chandler

In my opinion, the book you currently hold in your hand is one of the most concise and relevant in the market today. Giving this reading your full and undivided attention could be the most impactful financial decision you make this year. David Saucer has over two decades of experience in the financial services industry. His ability to communicate intricate financial ideas in a simple manner will make this book a very valuable resource.

The strategies and principles David delineates, while somewhat unknown to the majority, are those that have helped some of the most successful people in our country's success build their businesses. As you read, I think you'll find that the unconventional thoughts shared will begin to excite you as you see the vision of what's possible.

Unfortunately, there are many who will disregard or refuse to study what Mr. Saucer is giving. Many financial 'gurus', family members, friends, and colleagues will not understand how important these issues are. As you will soon appreciate, it is vital to keep an objective point of view while internalizing this material.

David A. Saucer

I can tell you one thing for sure—these ideas have changed my life. Yes, there are some who still do not understand, some individuals that I am (or was) very close to. Even so, the truth will set you free. Let the truth set you free.

B. Chase Chandler
Best-Selling Author of *The Wealthy Physician* and *The Wealthy Family*

# Introduction:
# Savings vs. Investing

The book you have in your hand will provide you with an understanding of a powerful savings strategy. Not an investment strategy, but a savings plan. The information enclosed is not about becoming extraordinarily wealthy—it's about being extraordinarily wise.

Think of this book as the start of a conversation. After reading this simple but profound bit of information, you will have the opportunity to see how this savings strategy could fit in your overall financial picture.

In Dwayne Burnell's *A Path to Financial Peace of Mind*, the author differentiates between *savings* and *investing*—terms that, over the years, have been used to describe a wide variety of financial products. We sometimes make the mistake of using the terms interchangeably, as though they mean the same thing. But saving and investing are two very distinct concepts. Your savings consist of money that you *cannot afford to lose*. Money you invest is money that is subject to the risk of loss.

Any money that you designate as savings should be in a financial vehicle with low risk, easy access, and no fear of loss of principal. Money in savings builds gradually and safely. To be clear: when you have money in the stock market, either directly or through an investment fund, the principle is subject to loss.

A solid financial strategy includes two distinct groups of money. There should be money that is saved and not subject to risk of loss, and there should be money that is invested. A proper financial strategy will have these two components clearly distinguished. Invested money has the potential for greater growth, but also has a greater risk of loss.

Over the years, we've met with thousands of individuals from all walks of life. Individuals in the beginning stages of their accumulation of assets and individuals who are now at the stage where the assets or being used for distribution. We are convinced that this savings strategy should be a piece in every person's financial puzzle.

However, this savings strategy may have a special significance for families. Intrigued? Read on!


David A. Saucer
2015

☐

# Chapter One: Objective Decisions and the Right Vehicle

People are pretty much the same, wherever you go. We share the same dreams and aspirations. We want to take care of our families. We want a chance to build something that lasts. And when we reach retirement age, we'd like to reward ourselves for a life of hard work and planning. And when we reach the end of life's journey, we want to leave something behind for those we love.

Simple dreams, really. The tragedy is, most people fail to reach these shared aspirations. According to *Forbes* magazine, the average American faces "the greatest retirement crisis in American history...too frail to work and too poor to retire." As of 2010, more than 75 percent of retirement-age Americans had less than $30,000 in their retirement accounts. Corporate pensions have been eliminated in many cases, and both public and private pensions are in jeopardy.

Ask yourself, if so many people share the same dreams, and share the same dismal results, exactly what are they doing wrong? Would it surprise you to know that most people make the same mistakes with money?

The financial market offers a ton of investment opportunities to consider. I have friends and clients whose chosen career paths involved working a job with the state government or a municipality. They all long for the day retirement comes. They worked specifically for the future and for the pension they would receive. But families have more at stake than a quiet job and a quieter retirement.

I've always looked for the most efficient way to lead my family to personal financial freedom and designing a predictable retirement (should we ever choose to retire).

My search has taken me all over the country; attending workshops, seminars, and reading hundreds of books. Long hours of study refined my understanding of the subject of financial freedom. In the pages that follow, I'm going to give you a condensed version of what I learned. Consider this a "conversation starter," for one of the most important discussions of your life.

What I discovered is a little unorthodox, which won't surprise you all that much (especially if you've been following my argument closely). The best solution to the problem of wealth building is not the most popular solution. If the popular solutions worked best, more people would reach their financial goals, and less would be facing a life of toil and poverty.

What we're talking about is the proper **financial vehicle**—a term that refers to a place to hold money and/or produce a return. A savings account is a financial vehicle. So are shares of stock. The metaphor of a *vehicle* is appropriate because we want our investments to "go somewhere" (like a comfortable retirement)!

The vehicle metaphor is even more useful when you make a direct comparison between choosing a car and financial choices. When you make a car purchase, what are the things you consider before buying? Not everyone considers the same things. For example, a young couple with an infant might rank safety pretty high on the list. A successful businessman may want a prestigious car. What options do you find important in a car?

- Safety
- Speed
- Handling
- A Track Record of Performance
- Low Operating Cost
- Efficiency

Likewise, we choose our financial vehicles with a list of options—in many cases, the same criteria as for your car!

- Safety - You don't want to lose your money overnight!
- Speed - How fast will your investment grow?
- Handling - You want control and use of your funds.
- A Track Record of Performance - Not a recent gimmick.
- Low Operating Cost – You want your financial vehicle to make money for you, not your financial advisor.
- Efficiency – You want advantageous tax treatment.

Of course, some people make both their car and their investment choices for **subjective** reasons, including feelings and emotions. A car looks cool, so it must be safe, right? The neighbors bought the same model as the man down the street. That means the car has low operating costs, right?

> *Everything in life is somewhere else; and you get there in a car.*
> E.B. White

I'm going to suggest that we use **objective** reasons instead—reasons which are based on historical data and hard facts. Over the course of this book, I will compare common financial vehicles and the features, options and benefits included in each one. That way, you can make an educated decision based on objective reasoning.

As you read, keep important investment criteria in mind. Do you want a fast, safe financial vehicle with a proven track record for success and durability? Or do you want to follow your neighbor's lead and hope he knows what he's doing?

# Chapter Two: Following the Herd

So why do so many people make the wrong investment and retirement decisions? If the majority of Americans reach retirement age unable to stop working, with nothing to pass on to their children but debt, why do so many people follow in their footsteps?

There's a simple answer to that question. Objective decision-making takes some work. You have to do a little reading. You have to seek out expert opinions. By contrast, *it's easy to follow the herd.*

**Herd behavior** is an interesting phenomenon. Suppose you're hungry, and you find yourself in front of two restaurants. Both look good. Which one should get your business? You could hook up a laptop or visit the library computer, do a search for reviews, and see what people think of the two restaurants.

But like I said, you're hungry. Really hungry!

Herding behaviors occur frequently in everyday decisions, based on observation or discussion with others. Suppose that earlier, when both restaurants were empty, the first customer of the evening chose the restaurant on the left at random. Later, a couple looks in both windows. The restaurant on the right is empty. They move back to the restaurant on the left. And so on, with other customers making an assumption of quality based on the size of the crowd. "They must know something," you think as you join the herd. This sort of collective behavior is called an **information cascade**—joining in the behavior of others through observation, despite personal preferences or knowledge.

> *Once the herd starts moving in one direction, it's hard to turn it, even slightly.*
> Dan Rather

Not that a decision like where to have dinner or what sports team to root for will affect the rest of your life. But what about choosing a financial vehicle? Do you really want to make a financial decision based on herd behavior? Birds and insects flock and swarm. Smart individuals decide things objectively!

Some herd decisions are born from habit. Sales guru Zig Ziglar tells a story that pertains to decision-making. He observed his wife cutting off the end of a ham before placing it into the oven to bake. He asked why she made the cut. She explained that she'd always baked a ham that way, and that her mother had always done the same. Did he not like the ham?

Sure, he told her. He was simply curious. But the curiosity didn't go away, and when he met his mother-in-law later in the week, he asked her about the ham. Her answer was much the same as his wife's: "My mother always cut off the end of the ham before baking." His wife's mother's mother was a great cook. If something worked for her, then it had to be the right thing to do.

Curiosity unsated, he resolved to ask the family matriarch. Yes, the old woman admitted; the end of the ham had to come off before baking. It seems that when she'd first married, she and her husband didn't have much money for kitchen equipment. The one baking pan they owned was small, and most hams wouldn't fit. So she'd cut off the end to make it fit.

The chances are good that your parents had a passbook savings account. Does that mean you're going to let passbook savings be the focus of your investment strategy? If you do, you may be cutting off more than just the end of your ham!

> *I stayed on my own path and did not follow the herd. I made a way for myself.*
> ~Eartha Kitt

What about public opinion? If there's a consensus, doesn't that fact indicate something? **Conventional wisdom** is the body of ideas that's accepted as truth by the public. *Conventional* means generally accepted. Orthodox. (Unoriginal.) *Wisdom* is a scholarly body of knowledge. Now here's a thought: Conventional thought is generally accepted without close objective examination. And wisdom is scholarly thought, examined closely and revised as new knowledge becomes available.

Doesn't it strike you that conventional, unexamined thought can't also be considered wisdom? That means "conventional wisdom" is an oxymoron—an inherently contradictory term, like *jumbo shrimp* and *heavy diet.*

The fact is, the progress of mankind can be marked by the mistaken notions of conventional wisdom, from the belief in a "flat earth" to the belief that the "stock market is safe." Nuggets of so-called conventional wisdom are not only unexamined, they are often dead wrong.

- In 1899, Charles Duell, an official at the U.S. Patent Office, noted, "Everything

that can be invented has been invented." Two years later, vacuum cleaners were invented. The year after that, air-conditioning.
- Lord Kelvin, President of the Royal Society, echoed popular sentiment when he said, "X-rays will prove to be a hoax."
- Thomas Watson, President of the Board at IBM, said, "I think there's a world market for maybe five computers."

Worse, conventional wisdom is often an obstacle to the acceptance of newly acquired information, to introducing new theories and explanations. "Wisdom" acts as a barrier that must be overcome by legitimate alternative views.

Will conventional wisdom stop you from realizing your full economic potential? What I'm arguing for here is a conscious, objective approach to the topics of investment and retirement planning. Strip away herd behavior and its close cousins, habit and consensus, and what's left is fact-based decision making. And that's a process you can bank on.

# Chapter Three: The Search for the Perfect Asset

As I said earlier, we will take an objective look at the most common financial vehicles in which we store our money. To list a few:

- Shoebox
- Stock Market
- Certificate of Deposit (CD)
- Money Market Account
- 401K / IRA
- Real Estate
- CA$H Residence/Private Economic System (PES)

You might find it funny that we listed a "shoebox" here. The other cliché you might have heard is "hiding your money in a mattress." Some people don't trust any investments at all. They figure that if they hold tight to their cash, they won't lose anything.

Are they right? No. Let me introduce another term: **opportunity costs**. Suppose you have a choice between working an extra shift at your job, and going to an amusement park. Going to the park will cost you $100. But that's not your only cost if you choose the amusement park. You pay to go to the park, and you lose the extra wages you might have otherwise earned. Opportunity costs are the loss of a potential gain from other choices when you settle on one alternative. In our example, if you settle on the amusement park, you pay to play, and you lose wages, too.

Look at our list of financial vehicles. Which ones carry hidden opportunity costs? (The answer may surprise you.)

But first, let's compare some of the positive features of each type of investment here. I encourage you to objectively compare the benefits that each financial vehicle carries:

Shoebox
- Safety
- Liquidity
- Control

Stock Market
- Liquidity
- High Contributions

C.D. (Certificate of Deposit)
- Safety
- High contributions
- Collateral opportunities
- No- loss provision

Money Market Account
- Safety
- High contributions
- Collateral opportunities
- No- loss provision

Real Estate
- Tax-deferred growth
- High contributions

CA$H Residence (PES)
- Tax-deferred growth
- TAX-FREE distribution (Tax-Free Retirement)
- High contribution limits
- Collateral opportunities
- Safety—Principle that is NEVER at risk
- Guaranteed loan options
- Unstructured loan payments
- Liquidity—use and control
- Heirs receive inheritance TAX-FREE

You might not be familiar with the last of the financial vehicles. The **Personal Economic System (PES)** is a financial vehicle with positive options that directly address some of the shortcomings of other financial vehicles.

What exactly are those shortcomings? We already mentioned opportunity costs inherent in the "shoebox" method of saving. The same holds true for passbook savings. If you can safely earn a higher rate of return elsewhere, you lose by selecting the lower rate. Opportunity costs are a concern.

A second concern is complexity. Investing in some financial vehicles is relatively easy. Most banks, for example, offer similar certificates of deposit. But investing in the stock market isn't nearly as simple. Stocks can be risky. Even the so-called experts who study the market for a living have a tough time predicting where the market is headed. And stocks aren't the only risky venture. If the real estate market takes a nosedive, you can find yourself stuck with property that's worth less than the mortgage!

**Liquidity** is another important consideration. Liquidity involves the availability of funds. Money in a shoebox is very liquid—you grab a handful and spend it! Other investments come under the heading of what I call a **money prison.** Many financial vehicles restrict your use of your own money! You can obtain funds from a certificate of deposit, for example, but you may pay substantial penalties for withdrawing funds outside of the original terms of the agreement. Real Estate can be a tremendous financial vehicle, but if our equity or cash is needed, you may have to sell the asset to use it. That can take weeks…or months.

For comparison's sake, let's look at an investment that the experts have been praising for decades—the 401 K plan. Conventional wisdom says that's the safest path to retirement. One thing's for sure—if you bank on a 401k, you won't be alone. The rest of the herd will be there with you. But let's take an objective look at the drawbacks to most 401k plans:

- Many plans are booby-trapped (full of hidden fees that can eat away your growth).
- Lack of control.
- Limited investment options.
- The specter of inflation haunts most long-term plans.

- Promotes false security (allowing bad spending habits and an increased debt tolerance).

> *To start off, I've never been a fan of the 401k…it's a real loser's bet if you think about it.*
> Daniel Ameduri

And you don't know what the future will bring. That means you can put your money into an IRA for 30 years and still not know how your financial future will end up. Do you remember the stock market crash of 2008? Can you imagine how people felt as they reached retirement age, only to read about the crash in the morning paper? Can you imagine losing a lifetime of planning just when you count most on the money?

# Chapter Four: The Usual Suspects

The 401K isn't the only gathering place for the herd. Let's take a few moments to look at popular savings and investment vehicles and see what they have to offer.

Conventional wisdom says you can count on the stock market to fund your retirement. In one form or another, 84 percent of Americans own stock at one time in their lives. Think about that statistic. That's a lot of people buying into a rollercoaster. Take a look at the chart that follows. Over a twelve year period beginning in the year 2000, the ups and downs added up to nothing. The Dow started at 12,000 and ended at 12,000. During the same time period, 31 percent inflation robbed investors of their buying power. The chart does indicate a clear winner—brokers charging transaction fees!

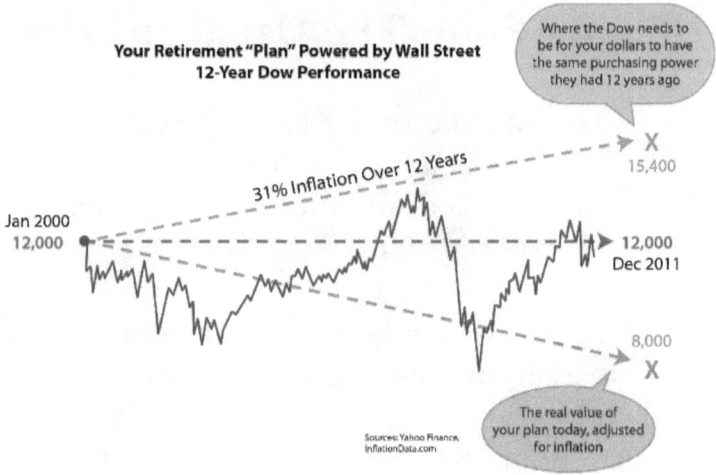

The truth is, there's a kind of excitement associated with buying and selling stocks, similar to the excitement of dice or a roulette wheel. To be fair, gambling is a zero-sum game (winners are matched to losers) that doesn't depend on production or profits. But casual investors have little or no chance to be successful. Experts weigh many factors before investing in a company, including:

- Capitalization
- Revenues
- Profits
- Competitors
- Industry trends
- Price to earnings ratios for both the company and its competitors
- Management

- Ownership
- Balance sheet analysis
- Stock price history
- Stock options
- Revenue and profit projections
- Industry risks
- Company risks

What happens if you beat the odds and your stock jumps in price? When you sell the stock, you pay capital gains tax. Or perhaps you hold onto the stock, praying that you can ride out the next market crash.

Professional, full-time investment experts may be willing to buy and sell stocks for you (for a fee), but in the end, their expertise will never come with a guarantee.

Mutual funds are a very popular financial vehicle. If you rely on results printed in the fund prospectus, though, you may be misled about what kind of results to expect:

- According to the *Hulbert Financial Digest*, 80 percent of mutual funds perform below their benchmarks.
- Funds only advertise only "buy-and-hold" results (ten years or more), despite the fact that the average fund investor holds on to

the fund for five years or less. For that reason, most investors don't capture the results promoted in sales brochures.

- The fund industry hopes investors won't mind a one percent fee rate. But according to the Department of Labor, a fund charging that fee rate over a 35-year period will devour 28 percent of your savings (assuming an annual return rate of seven percent).

- Comparing the results between mutual companies using three to five year increments is ineffective. According to the *Hulbert Financial Digest*, a 15-year track record is necessary to eliminate blind luck as a factor in performance evaluation. Given a sufficient track record, the fund industry's glaring performance holes are clearly visible.

Another common financial strategy involves relying on home equity as the centerpiece of a retirement plan. Unfortunately, real estate offers another rollercoaster ride. The U.S. home market peaked in 2006, and the subsequent fall wiped out a decade's worth of gains. In the meantime, inflation eroded real value, leaving homeowners on the short end of the stick. And, as with stocks, the sale of a home results in capital gains taxes that eat any real profits.

Discouraging, isn't it? Easy to see why the average head of household in his or her sixties has only saved a quarter of what's needed for retirement!

Detailing the shortcomings of various investment assets is easier than explaining why one particular asset is superior to others. To understand why the CA$H Residence Personal Economic System (PES) has advantages over other strategies, you need to fully understand two issues—taxation and interest compounding. In the next two chapters, we'll briefly discuss those concepts. Then we'll talk more about the perfect asset!

# Chapter Five: Financial Assets and Taxation

One financial axiom advises, *Taxes affect financial decisions.* Proponents of the IRA note that 401k plans defer taxes. Is that really a benefit? Let's look at how taxes affect investments, including the difference between *tax deferred* and *tax exempt.*

*The tax man cometh* is a phrase which puts fear in the hearts of many. We all must pay taxes, and if you achieve any financial success, your share of the tax burden will be greater than others.

We always ask our clients, "What do you think? Are taxes going up or down?" In my experience, 100 percent of the people we asked think that taxes are going up. How could they think otherwise? All governments overspend. But what's disappointing is, taxes can go up with the single stroke of a pen and a new law. Without warning, lawmakers can change the rules and we are required to play by them.

With that kind of game, how can you win? Forget winning—how can you plan?

Based on current law, we do have some options to minimize the tax burden if we think ahead and implement a detailed plan. But when sorting possibilities, ask yourself, "Am I paying tax on the seed or the harvest?" Let me explain.

The Gospels share over 40 parables. In many of them, Jesus uses an understanding of agriculture to deliver his message. Likewise, I would like to use an analogy using a farmer and his corn harvest to explain a problem with tax-deferred financial vehicles.

In the beginning of the season, the farmer prepares the ground, plants the seed and dreams of an abundant harvest. In some years, the harvest is plentiful. In other years, the farmer is disappointed. When a person decides to put a portion of their income into an IRA, they will get the tax deduction for the current year and pray for an abundant harvest at retirement.

But after due diligence, you may find that an IRA may not be the best choice. If the farmer had the option to pay the tax on the seed or pay the tax on the harvest, which would he choose? I submit that in most cases, he would choose to pay the tax on the seed. By the time the harvest comes in, taxes may have gone up. In both the Roth IRA and in the CA$H Residence system, we choose to pay the taxes on the seed.

There are three tax strategies for your retirement:
- Taxable

- Tax-deferred
- Tax-free

These three strategies will have an impact on your taxes; either today's taxes or tomorrow's taxes! Let's take a closer look at each of these three options:

**Taxable -** You pay tax now and invest with after-tax dollars. Then, you pay tax on all the earnings *as they are earned.* (Returning to our parable, this is like paying taxes on both the seed and on the harvest as it grows!) These investments include non-qualified accounts such as savings accounts, CDs, stocks, and bonds.

**Tax-deferred** - You get a tax deduction now and invest with pre-tax dollars. You won't pay tax on the earnings until you use them. (This is like paying taxes on the whole harvest later.) These investments include qualified accounts, such as a Traditional IRA and most pension plans. There are limits to how much you can contribute, and you are required to take the money out after the age of seventy and pay taxes. (Remember our earlier question—will taxes be higher or lower in the future?)

**Tax-free -** You pay tax now (on the seed) and never pay taxes on the harvest. This is a ROTH IRA or the cash value in a life insurance policy.

The ROTH IRA is limited to individuals under a certain income, whereas the life insurance contributions can be much higher.

But which path is best? That depends on the future of taxes. Let's look at some scenarios:

## What if Tax Rates Stay the Same?

If tax rates stay the same, it doesn't matter if you pay tax now (on the seed) or later (on the harvest). The final outcome is the same, believe it or not:

| Tax Rate Remains Constant (35%) 7% Growth for 20 years | | Tax on Seed | Tax on Harvest | Gain/ Loss |
|---|---|---|---|---|
| | Investment | 100,000 | 100,000 | |
| | After Tax | 65,000 | | |
| | Future Value | 251,570 | 387,030 | |
| | Less Tax | 0 | <135,460> | |
| | Future Investment | $251,570 | $251,570 | $0 |

## What if Tax Rates Go Down?

If tax rates go down, you would be better off paying tax on the harvest. In this scenario, you would save $27,100 by investing in your IRA or qualified accounts:

| Tax Rate Decrease (35% to 28%) 7% Growth for 20 years | | Tax on Seed | Tax on Harvest | Gain/ Loss |
|---|---|---|---|---|
| | Investment | 100,000 | 100,000 | |
| | After Tax | 65,000 | | |
| | Future Value | 251,570 | 387,030 | |
| | Less Tax | 0 | <108,360> | |
| | Future Investment | $251,570 | $278,670 | $27,100 |

## What if Tax Rates Go Up?

If tax rates go up, you would be better off paying tax on the seed. By investing in your ROTH IRA or your permanent life insurance policy, you could have saved $27,100.

| Tax Rate Increase (35% to 42 %) 7% Growth for 20 years | | Tax on Seed | Tax on Harvest | Gain/ Loss |
|---|---|---|---|---|
| | Investment | 100,000 | 100,000 | |
| | After Tax | 65,000 | | |
| | Future Value | 251,570 | 387,030 | |
| | Less Tax | 0 | <162,560> | |
| | Future Investment | $251,570 | $224,470 | <$27,1000> |

So what's the best path? Since we can't see the future, there's no certainty. We don't know where the tax rates will be in the future. We don't know who will be elected, and what legislation they will enact.

However, we do know that the government has hefty obligations. Social Security, Medicare and other programs must be funded. The country is, at the time of publication, $17 *trillion* in debt. Our government is already struggling to fund programs in today's dollars and our obligations may well grow exponentially.

The government's main source of income is taxation, and additional funding could very well come from future tax increases.

What is the best course of action? Planning! In order to properly prepare for retirement and your taxes, having a plan that maximizes the potential for you to reach your goals, while minimizing taxes is best.

**Important!** The examples in this chapter are hypothetical, and should not be taken as specific tax or investment advice. There are no guarantees in any investment return or tax rate. But having your assets placed in ways that minimize your taxes now and in the future will be critical as the tax rates change.

So I'll ask you again: Do you think taxes will go up or down?

# Chapter Six: The Phenomenon of Compound Interest

**Compound interest** is interest added to the principal of an investment so that the added interest also earns interest. The addition of interest to the principal, allowing additional interest accrual, is called compounding.

Mathematically speaking, the formula below expresses compound interest. P is the original principle and X is the rate of interest expressed as a decimal. At the end of the nth year, the compounded amount will be:

$$P (1 + X) n$$

> *Compound interest is the eighth wonder of the world. He who understands it, earns it ... he who doesn't ... pays it.*
> ~Albert Einstein

Confused? Understand this: the growth of the compound amount—the total value of your investment—is exponential, not linear. But that only works if you have uninterrupted compounding. To understand exponential growth, let's review an old riddle: Would you rather I give you $1,000,000 dollars or a Penny a day doubled for 31 days? A million dollars would be great, but if I understand the phenomenon of uninterrupted compounding and exponential growth, I would make a different choice.

| Doubling a Penny for 30 Days | |
|---|---|
| Day 1    $.01 | Day 16 $327.68 |
| Day 2    $.02 | Day 17 $655.36 |
| Day 3    $.04 | Day 18 $1,310.72 |
| Day 4    $.08 | Day 19 $2,621.44 |
| Day 5    $.16 | Day 20 $5,242.88 |
| Day 6    $.32 | Day 21 $10,485.76 |
| Day 7    $.64 | Day 22 $20,971.52 |
| Day 8    $1.28 | Day 23 $41,943.04 |
| Day 9    $2.56 | Day 24 $83,886.08 |
| Day 10 $5.12 | Day 25 $167,772.16 |
| Day 11 $10.24 | Day 26 $335,544.32 |
| Day 12 $20.48 | Day 27 $671,088.64 |
| Day 13 $40.96 | Day 28 $1,342,177.28 |
| Day 14 $81.92 | Day 29 $2,684,354.56 |
| Day 15 $163.84 | Day 30 $5,368,709.12 |

So which is it? $1,000,000 or $ 5,368,709

Uninterrupted compound interest is an amazing phenomenon that works best when given additional time. For that reason, it's particularly important to start early. The CA$H Residence is most effective for young savers, allowing exponential growth its full course.

Perhaps you recall the Biblical parable of the talents. A wealthy man entrusted a number of talents (a monetary unit worth 20 years in wages) to his servants. One servant received five talents, another two, and a third servant received one talent. When the man returned from his journeys, he asked each servant what they'd done with the money he'd left with them. The servant who'd shepherded five talents had invested them, and doubled his talents—he now had ten. The servant who had two talents had doubled his as well—he now had four talents. The servant who had one talent had taken it and buried it in the ground, untouched. He still had the one talent, intact—but he'd done nothing to increase his wealth.

> Proverbs 13:11
> *Dishonest money dwindles away, but whoever gathers money little by little makes it grow.*

Then, the wealthy man did something unexpected. He took the single talent and gave it to the servant who already had ten, admonishing, "Thou wicked and slothful servant!" The lesson is clear. Even the Bible worries over opportunity costs! And though we all start with different circumstances, and all end up with different results, *it's what we do with what we have that matters.*

Scripture is clear on the subject of wealth. Riches are a gift from God, to be used in His service. We are stewards, encouraged to increase the blessing through investment and directed toward generosity to others.

Continuous compounding is a wealth creation strategy that allows you to be a wise steward of the gifts in your life. So, are you going to bury your money in the ground, or put it where it can do the most good?

# Chapter Seven: Inside the CA$H Residence

So what is the CA$H Residence Personal Economic System (PES)? Simply put, this set of oft-neglected financial assets comes under the heading of **cash value life insurance**.

Cash value life insurance? It's been around for centuries. Edmund Halley, the astronomer who discovered Halley's Comet, also developed the first actuarial table. His work was continued by James Dodson, the 18th century mathematician, leading to the first life insurance company, founded in London.

In the Americas, the first life insurance ventures were spearheaded by Presbyterian and Episcopalian churches. When the massacre of George Armstrong Custer at the Battle of the Little Bighorn stranded a number of families in the West, public sentiment for the protection afforded by life insurance gave birth to a vibrant new industry.

Cash value life insurance—your CA$H Residence (PES) solution—is a financial asset that offers insurance protection, but also accumulates cash value during the policyholder's lifetime. This is a personalized economic system with a stunning array of benefits, including:

- Tax-Deferred growth
- TAX-FREE Distribution (Tax-Free Retirement)
- Competitive returns
- High Contribution limits
- Collateral Opportunities
- Principle that is NEVER at Risk
- Interest that is Guaranteed
- Guaranteed Loan options
- Unstructured Loan payments
- Liquidity, Use and Control
- Safety
- Heirs receive inheritance Tax- Free

The CA$H Residence (PES) fits the criteria of the perfect savings asset. But you'll find that it's so much more than that. When we refer to a personal economic system, we're talking about aspects you may never have considered. Let's take a closer look at these possibilities.

## Generational Wealth

One aspect of the CA$H Residence strategy that we've not yet discussed is the possibility for building *generational wealth*. We're all familiar with generational poverty, so difficult for the modern family to escape. But instead of a vicious cycle of poverty and meager entitlements, what if we were empowered to not only better our circumstances, but start a pattern of wealth-building that continued on to our children and our children's children? That's what using a tax-free distribution is about!

> *When I was young I thought that money was the most important thing in life; now that I am old I know that it is.*
> ~Oscar Wilde

The *gift that keeps on giving* is a phrase that applies to the CA$H Residence. Properly structuring a life insurance contract through a series of gifted premium payments allows you to provide grandchildren with substantial educational and financial opportunities. Because the savings are tax-deferred and accumulate within the account policy, the cash value can be used for various purposes, including college education, a business opportunity or even a down payment on a home. Furthermore, the cash value can be used to supplement retirement income later in the grandchild's life. Would you like to permanently affect the financial trajectory of your family? The CA$H Residence may be the perfect asset for you.

## Become Your Own Banker

In general, there are three kinds of people in the world: *spenders, savers,* and *bankers.* Spenders live check to check at the mercy of creditors. Spenders make high-ticket purchases, but they pledge their future earnings to make those purchases. Savers are smarter. They set aside money for future purchases. But when they use their savings, they lose their compound interest forever. Savers assume that their diligence guarantees a brighter future. Is that really so?

> Proverbs 22:7
> *The rich rule over the poor, and the borrower is slave to the lender.*

Bankers, on the other hand, never interrupt the miracle of compound interest. They make high-ticket purchases using other people's money. When business opportunities arise, they fund them without cutting the future short. And the good news is, you don't need a job at a bank to be that kind of banker!

There are some purchases that require financing. Houses, cars and education are simply too expensive to purchase with cash. Do you have a mortgage? Credit cards? If so, you're already aware of the problem. The majority of Americans pay 30 to 40 percent of their money to someone else's bank.

The revolutionary idea that you could become your own banker owes much to R. Nelson Nash, the financial genius behind *Infinite Banking*. Instead of giving your money to another bank to use, why not finance major purchases with your own money, tax-free? Nash envisioned building a personal economic system—the CA$H Residence—that would allow you to do just that.

Looking for a loan? While money is still compounding inside a whole life policy, the insurance company will let you **collateralize** (borrow from) your policy and make you a loan. They do this without any financial application. When you are your own banker, the loan doesn't need an approval process. All you have to do is ask for the loan, and it's yours.

## IRS Section 7702

Money inside a whole life insurance policy resides in a completely different section of the income tax code than IRAs and 401k plans. Since 1985, Section 7702 is where the tax freedom still exists and why billions are currently pouring into this area.

Prior to 1985, the government kept a hands-off approach to taxing life insurance policies. The reason for this was political—they didn't want to be seen as taxing widows and children. However, the financial world began promoting investments as "life insurance" to avoid paying taxes. Section 7702 was created to limit the tax-free benefits to genuine life insurance policies.

Looking for tax diversification for your portfolio? The CA$H Residence provides tax-free payments to your beneficiaries, tax-free loans and gifts, and cash for retirement without the "harvest tax" that's hidden in an IRA or 401k.

## A Universal Benefit

So far, we've taken steps to understand the problem of wealth-building and explain why so many share the dream yet fail to attain it. We've taken an objective look at traditional savings and investment strategies in our search for the perfect asset. And we've introduced you to an old strategy that is too often overlooked by the average American. The CA$H Residence (PES) can be of benefit to *everyone*.

# Chapter Eight: What Do the Experts Know?

Suppose there was an institution that gathered the greatest minds in the financial world. Economists, accountants, financial analysts and attorneys, all under one roof, all focused on the efficient use of money. You'd want to know how they invested the institution's capital, wouldn't you? You'd want to know what the experts behind-the-scenes do to maximize growth and stability while reducing taxes.

### Banks and Cash Value Life Insurance

If there's one institution that really understands the use of cash value life insurance, it's banks. These financial institutions are involved in most every aspect of our economy. Commercial banks hold billions of dollars inside cash value life insurance policies. It's one of their greatest secrets. Why do they hold so much? Banks want to insure their future profitability and existence. Banks enjoy the tax-free accumulation of the cash values. What better way to fund employee healthcare, pensions and other benefits than with a safe, time-tested strategy?

Nearly every major bank makes their balance sheet public, according to FDIC rules and regulations. Take a look at just how much money some well-known banks hold in life insurance.

| Banking Institution | Life Insurance Assets |
|---|---|
| Bank of America | $19,607,000,000 |
| Wells Fargo Bank | $17,739,000,000 |
| J.P. Morgan Chase Bank | $10,327,000,000 |
| U. S. Bank | $5,451,892,000 |

Banks place billions of dollars into life insurance. Is that important? You bet it is. Banks are in the money business. Placing their money in cash value life insurance is so common, financial experts have coined jargon to describe it, including "bank-owned life insurance" (BOLI). When corporations do the same, it's called "corporate-owned life insurance" (COLI).

The FDIC allows Life Insurance Assets to be classified as *Tier 1* capital—the safest capital. The amount of Tier 1 capital a bank has is considered to be a good measure of the bank's financial strength and stability. The Office of The Comptroller of The Currency advocates life insurance as an asset by making insurance part of the banking laws. Up to 25 percent of commercial banks' Tier 1 operating capital can be invested in life insurance.

**Case Studies**

Another way to approach the question, "What do the experts know?" is to look for a track record of how a particular option worked out for people in the past. Let's take a look back at some famous, respected entrepreneurs and the companies they founded, and see what the role of cash value life insurance played in their success.

## Nearly Wiped Out

The stock market crash of 1929 destroyed a lot of companies. One chain of dry goods stores, supplying important goods to mining and farm families, was particularly hard hit. The owner suffered from the effects of great physical and mental strain. And his company was nearly wiped out.

 What saved John Cash Penney was his cash value life insurance policies. At a time of desperate need, he was able to borrow against those policies to pay his employees and keep his company running. After the Great Depression, the company—J.C. Penney—was able to rebound and become one of the greatest retail companies in the country. Today, the company boasts more than 1,100 stores worldwide, doing $18 billion a year in sales.

## An Icon is Born

Ray was one of three partners who dreamed of creating a hamburger empire. The other two partners sold out after six years, though the chain still bears their name. Meanwhile, Ray built the company despite almost constant cash-flow problems.

Anyone who knows about rapid business growth knows that sometimes, companies grow *too* fast. The bills can pile up quicker than the revenues, and suddenly, the success story is over. Ray was smart, though, and for the first eight years, he didn't even take a salary. When times were tough, he helped cover the salaries of key employees by borrowing against his cash value life insurance policies.

Ray Kroc believed in the power of advertising. Though it's not well known, Ray also used his cash value life insurance to help finance a marketing campaign featuring a clown that would become a fixture in American pop culture— Ronald McDonald. The rest is history.

Today, McDonalds serves more than 50 million people a day at more than 30,000 locations across the globe.

## A Clean Amusement Park

Back in the day, amusement parks were pretty shady places. Carneys ran run-down attractions, rip-off "games of skill" and dangerous rides. Walter had a vision for a family-friendly amusement park that catered to the hopes and dreams of children. Needless to say, investors didn't fall over themselves to give Walter—a cartoonist turned entrepreneur—the money he needed.

The vision was unique. Walter told a friend, "I want it to look like nothing else in the world. And it should be surrounded by a train." After five years of planning, the project was launched. What many people don't know is, Walt Disney helped finance *Disneyland* and other projects with cash value life insurance policies.

Think of what an impact Disneyland has had on our culture! Our whole perception of amusement parks has changed, thanks to the vision of the man who gave us feature-length cartoons, television shows and, of course, a certain mouse…

## From Typhoid to Tutelage

Leland and Jane lost a son to typhoid fever, a devastating disease that plagued mankind for centuries (typhoid once wiped out a third of the population in ancient Athens, Greece). To compensate for the loss of their son, the couple decided to dedicate their lives to helping other people's children. They founded a University, and enrolled 555 students in just the first year.

Then, tragedy struck again. Leland died just two years after the university's founding, leaving Jane with financial struggles and the prospect of a failed enterprise.

But Jane would not give up on the dream. She was able to survive six years of fragile finances with the proceeds from her husband's cash value life insurance. The faculty was paid and operations continued uninterrupted.

Today, Stanford University, Leland and Jane Stanford's dream, boasts more than 15,000 students, both graduate and undergraduate. The university is one of the most respected schools in the country.

## What's Cooking?

Doris had been a Tupperware salesperson, and was actually pretty successful at it. The business model seemed sound. But wouldn't she be even more successful running a company of her own, using a similar model?

Doris believed that some of the cooking tools available to women in the home were inferior to the ones available to chefs in restaurants. She imagined success selling professional-quality cooking products in-home, using the "sales party" techniques she'd learned. Using her cash value life insurance policy, Doris funded a company that started in her basement and became a national phenomenon.

Today, Pampered Chef is a billion-dollar enterprise with more than 12 million customers. Doris Christopher turned a dream and a vision into a fortune.

But not without financial help.

America is experiencing a life insurance renaissance, fueled by individuals with financial wealth who seek to protect their money from the Government and look to diversify to mitigate the risk of Wall Street volatility and uncertainty.

Armed with contracts that guarantee safety and performance (something Wall Street cannot and will not do), the wealthy put their money in cash value insurance.

## Chapter Nine: The Private Reserve Account

The **Private Reserve Account** is a cash value life insurance policy that pays a tax-free death benefit, but also pays dividends that increase the policy's cash value. That cash value has unique advantages. We've been calling this kind of account the CA$H Residence. Next, we're going to zero in on the benefits of this asset, which allows you to be your own banker and guide your own financial destiny.

First, let's take a moment to see how insurance works. Insurance companies begin with a statistical model on a large population data base, making certain to include people of all ages. An **actuarial**—a person who computes risk based on statistical information—develops the model. Next, a **rate maker** takes the information and determines what a company will have to charge in order to meet death claim obligations. Once rates are set, lawyers create legal, binding contracts that are offered to the public through a sales force. The insurance company creates an administrative group to oversee the whole system.

Take a moment to think about this. The insurance company doesn't own the contract. The owner of the contract is you. The insurance company promises to do certain things as long as you meet acceptability standards and make your premium payments. Those premium payments are "put to work," in order to produce the benefits promised. Insurance companies invest in conservative financial instruments (bonds, mortgages), and to a lesser extent, real estate or joint ventures.

Because you own the contract (policy), you outrank all other stakeholders in the process. You have first option to use the money at an agreed upon interest rate.

At the end of the year, the insurance company directors ask, "How did we do in comparison to the assumptions made by the actuaries and rate makers?" Based on that comparison, a dividend may be declared. That dividend is *not* taxable.

Why not? Let's look at an example. Suppose you buy a policy would require $1,000 a year to meet obligations. Several factors may alter the actual cost of that policy. Administrative costs may go up or down. More or fewer death benefits may have to be paid. Earnings may vary from estimates as well. Knowing this, the insurance company charges $1,100 a year. The extra "fudge factor" helps keep the system safe.

When the directors meet, they discover that the policy you purchased only cost $800 a year to maintain. Now, they have a decision to make about the surplus. In this case, the directors place $200 in a contingency fund, and return the remaining $100 as a dividend.

So why is the dividend not taxable? Technically, the dividend isn't a gain—it's a "return of premium." Unlike stock shares, which may lose value if the stock falls, the dividend can't lose value. You will use the dividend to purchase *paid up insurance* (which does not cost a sales commission or fees), thus increasing the tax-deferred accumulation of cash value.

Insurance policies are designed to become more efficient over time. Over the life of the policy, the cash value is guaranteed to reach the face amount of the policy. As dividends are applied, the insurance company faces an ever-decreasing "net amount of risk." The news is filled with stories of financial institutions (including Wall Street) that leave widows and children penniless. When was the last time you read about a life insurance company that failed to meet its obligations? Instances are statistically insignificant, for reasons we've just explored.

## Banking on Yourself

Now that you understand the process, we can talk about the advantages of the private reserve account. The essential idea of the account is to recover the interest you might normally pay to banking institutions through the use of dividend-paying life insurance, and then lending those funds to others so that the policy owner makes the money that a banking institution does. Funds may be lent to any party (including your-self) and earnings grow within the policy, tax-deferred. Thus, you are both reducing your tax burden and capturing monies for yourself that a banking institution normally would normally receive.

Anytime you can cut the payment of interest to others and direct that same market rate of interest to an entity you own and control, subject to minimal taxation, then you will have improved your wealth-generating potential significantly.

## It's About Financing

We're not talking about investing here. In the introduction to this book, we discussed investing verses saving. Here, we're talking about **financing**—providing funding for a person or enterprise. Financing involves both the creation and maintenance of a pool of money and its use.

What makes the Private Reserve Account special is that when a financing system is combined with an investment system, the combination will always outperform an investment system. And when the system combines a financing engine with reduced tax liability, allowing you to maintain complete control, the result is an ideal system.

Let's see how the system works. Suppose you plan to buy a car. You might finance it. When you're done paying off the principle and interest, the bank has your interest money and you have an old car. Or perhaps you'll lease the car. The payments will be less, but you won't own the old car when the lease ends—the bank will. Can you win by paying cash? No interest, right? No interest for the bank—or for you. Instead of building wealth, your money is gone.

Now imagine financing a car with your own money, borrowed from the private reserve account, which is still accumulating interest, even though the money is "in use." By becoming your own source of financing, you beat the banks at their own game!

> *The avoidance of taxes is the only intellectual pursuit that still carries any reward.*
> John Maynard Keynes, Economist

I think we can agree that we are all involved in elements of finance. If you pay interest to anyone else, or give up interest that could have been yours (opportunity costs), you are financing something. All the more reason to become your own banker! Between your occupation and your role as banker, which is more important? Consider the following:

- Americans spend a large portion of their annual income on interest expense.
- In addition, the average American spends about $0.30 of every dollar on taxes.

Now, if you're paying half of every dollar on taxes and interest, then your personal wealth would be greatly influenced by any strategy that captures interest while limiting tax liabilities, right? In fact, the impact would be greater than identifying good investments with high rates of return!

But what about families? What about the CA$H Residence is of particular value to them? Read on!

# Chapter Ten: The CA$H Residence and Families

I speak now from personal experience. For many years now, in both my writing and consultation of individuals, I used a particular phrase frequently: *My greatest calling is to be a dad.*

In all my years, there has never been a greater calling than the opportunity to be a father to my children. That role has been the greatest joy of my life. My wife and I are blessed with a safe home. Cindy and I are committed to keeping our home a sanctuary.

From a Biblical perspective, I have a mandate to be the provider and the protector of our home. The sanctuary we cherish isn't free. We have to work for it.

---

### 1 Timothy 5:8
*If anyone fails to provide for his relatives, and especially for those of his own family, he has disowned the faith and is worse than an unbeliever.*

---

I am fully aware that God is our source, the source of everything. He sees a sparrow when it flies and when it falls, and is certainly aware of my successes and failures. But from a Biblical perspective, the Word declares that I should be wise and a good steward, both of my time *and* my finances.

---

**Proverbs 13:22**

*A good man leaves an inheritance to his children's children. And the wealth of the sinner is stored up for the righteous.*

---

In previous chapters, I've written about the opportunities that the CA$H Residence offers. For a father taking on family responsibilities, taking direction from scripture, the benefits are obvious. But are there other benefits that families ought to consider?

- Between a mortgage, car loan, credit cards and other debt, most Americans face decades of debt! What would it mean to you to be completely out of debt in 10 years or less? That's possible when you are your own banker!
- Do you have children who'd like to go to college? The average cost of a single year in college is nearly $23,000. Funds from a policy grow tax-deferred. A policy taken

out on the life of a young child accumulates cash value for a relatively small premium. When it's time for college, the funds can be borrowed, keeping the policy in force.

- What if your child wants to supplement his education with student loans? Cash value life insurance is one of the few assets not considered in federal college financial aid calculations!

- The CA$H Residence offers the possibility of generational wealth. That is, you can create legacy opportunities. Want to provide your children and grandchildren with a stake in the future? Perhaps you want to provide a favored charity with a legacy gift. It's all possible with cash value life insurance.

The CA$H Residence offers value to nearly everyone. But for families, there's more at stake. Are you beginning to see the possibilities? Read on!

# Chapter Eleven: Case Studies

**Cody Woodrow** is a cook for a popular restaurant chain. Years over a hot grill gave him what he needs in the way of expertise. Cody doesn't mind the long hours and sweat, because when he goes home to his wife and daughter, his life is simple and blessed. Cody and his wife are amateur photographers, so Cody's days off are spent looking for interesting photo subjects. Their eight year-old daughter May loves to tag along.

Not long into her schooling, it becomes clear that May is gifted. Her grades are consistently excellent, and her achievement tests are off the charts. Cody never went to college, but he's determined that May will have that opportunity.

He fills out a personal financial plan, and after evaluating options that fit his limited income, he chooses cash value life insurance. A career in food service leaves little room for financial error. Cody opts for the absolute safety of a cash value policy.

Paying a premium of $250 a month, Cody will invest a total of $105,000 between the ages of 32 and 67. His payout after retirement, spread over 20 years, will be $371,185! More important, though, is the opportunity to borrow against his cash value to allow May to go to the college of her choice. It's too soon to know what field of study May will pursue, but it's not too soon to plan her financial options!

**Trevor Kaine** buys and "flips" houses for a living. His success depends on a number of varied skills and attributes, including a background in home inspections, an ability to research, and a seemingly endless well of patience (Trevor invests time in dozens of properties before buying one). When he finds a property that he knows he can make a profit on, his background in construction becomes a huge personal asset. At age 37, he's living the dream— success in business, a beautiful wife and three children.

Because he's made his money in real estate, Trevor has a healthy respect for the volatility of the market. People make fortunes…and they lose them. Trevor wants to put the money he's made someplace safe. As a responsible family man, he views their safety as his primary duty.

Trevor and his wife Rose evaluate their finances and make the decision to take out a cash value policy with a big monthly premium. Trevor pays $2,500 every month. If he retires at 67—30 years from now—what will he have paid in? What will his policy be worth?

All told, Trevor will have invested $900,000 in his CA$H Residence. At the end of 30 years, that investment will yield a 20-year annuity, with an annual payout of $122,999—a total of $3,817,900 (tax free).

Of course, nothing ever goes *exactly* as planned. When the three kids reach their teen years, the driveway becomes home to a *lot* of cars! Because Trevor is his own banker, he arranges his own loans without interrupting the continuous compounding of his cash value. And when it comes time for a second honeymoon, the trip to Europe is no problem. No matter how many houses Trevor owns, his CA$H Residence will certainly be his most important residence!

**Jazmine Owens** is a single mother with a young son. Jerome likes to play sports (especially hockey), watch television and hang with his friends. Mom works as a bookkeeper for the city and supplements her income by teaching classes online. On the weekends, mom watches her son compete in school sports, so they have a busy life.

Then one night, Jazmine's father asks about her finances. He's not being nosey—he's just looking ahead. Jazmine lives a comfortable life, so at first, she's a little taken back by her dad's questions. Driving home, she looks at her son and realizes that being "comfortable" just isn't enough.

After researching all of the possibilities, Jazmine decides to buy a cash value life insurance policy. She plans to retire at 65. What will his choice mean in terms of dollars?

Jazmine pays a $1,000 per month premium— using most of her second job's income. They have to "tighten the belt" a little, but that's not so bad. Over 25 years, her payments mean an investment of $300,000. (Of course, Jazmine has access to tax-free loans from his policy, which she takes advantage of when she learns how much it costs for a young man to play hockey in high school!)

When Jazmine retires, her death benefit has a value of $712,952. But she's alive and well, enjoying a life on the road (her son will become a professional hockey coach!) That life is fueled, in part, by an annual payout of $59,720 over 25 years.

# Chapter Twelve: Starting the Conversation

This book has been about starting a conversation. Chances are, you have been all too aware of the problems inherent in wealth-building. Perhaps you have experience with some of the traditional solutions—those favored by the herd. Now, you have a glimpse at an underappreciated asset that has the potential to change your life—a vehicle that can get you where you want to go.

It's my opinion that the private reserve account should be the foundation for every American's personal finance strategy. To explain why, let me use an analogy. In the days of westward expansion, settlers often trusted the transfer of their personal belongings to a Conestoga wagon—heavy, a heavy, cloth-covered wagon designed to travel across all kinds of terrain. Sturdy, iron-rimmed wheels were central to the success of the wagon. Each wheel featured a hub and a number of spokes, giving support to as much as 12,000 pounds of cargo! Along the way, spokes might break, but with a rock-solid hub, the wheel would continue to serve its purpose.

Let me ask you: what is the hub of your financial wheel? If your life's journey takes you through rough terrain, will your wheel continue to turn?

In the introduction to this book, I differentiated between savings and investments. The private reserve account is the perfect savings strategy— the sturdy, dependable hub everyone needs. Spokes—other investments from stocks to real estate—may break along the way. But if the hub is solid, you can still move forward.

So, what next?

The journey to financial freedom is a path many look for and never find. I'm talking about freedom from the shackles of normalcy and mediocrity. Freedom from fear and uncertainty. Freedom from the herd. Life is about launching into the unknown and breaking free. This relentless pursuit is seen in the drive and actions of entrepreneurs and dreamers.

> *Be sure you're right, then go ahead.*
> David Crockett, Frontiersman

Think back to the early history of this country. Can you imagine the drive of the earliest pioneers, who left everything behind and headed west without maps, without guides? They packed their belongings, taking only what was necessary, and forged ahead in search of a dream. And their friends and family? Most stayed behind.

*SWSWSW* is an acronym I frequently use in training and workshops. The acronym is an attitude and mindset which must be adopted.

*Some Will, Some Won't; So What?* Can you remove yourself from the expectations of those around you and set out on your own?

> *My interest is in the future because I am going to spend the rest of my life there.*
> ~Charles Kettering

Let me challenge you to reach for your dreams. Maximize your potential. Give your family the future they deserve. You're at a fork in the road, my friend. Will you follow the disappointed crowd, or will you choose the road less traveled?

Consider the conversation started!

# Appendix A: Life Insurance—an Overview

The CA$H Residence (PES) approach to building wealth specifies cash value life insurance. But there's more than one kind of life insurance. What are the different types, and how do they differ?

*Term Life Insurance* pays a benefit to survivors in the event of the death of an insured person. Policies are in force for a set period of time. When the policy expires, it's up to the insured party to purchase another policy. Term life has no investment component.

*Whole Life Insurance* combines a death benefit with an investment component. The cash value of the policy builds, tax-deferred, until the policy matures. You can borrow money against that accumulation, tax-free. Whole life is a *cash value life insurance,* as described in this book.

*Universal Life Insurance* combines a death benefit with a money-market type investment for a higher rate of return. Unlike cash value (whole life), the higher rate of return cannot be guaranteed because it's tied to stocks and bonds that involve risk.

# Appendix B: A Personal Plan for Financial Success

In my work for the financial industry, I've found that most people have already done some financial planning. Maybe they have some investments and some insurance. Perhaps they have employee benefits, or even a will. What they don't have is an understanding of how all of the pieces fit together.

A properly trained financial strategist will work on what they call the offensive and defensive sides of planning. The offensive side consists of savings, wealth accumulation and entrepreneurial ventures. The defensive side involves protecting against risk. The CA$H Residence attends to both the offensive and defensive.

Another aspect to consider involves the evolution of thinking. Simply put, you don't think the same way when you're 80 years old as when you're 25. We consistently hear older clients ask, "Why didn't someone explain this to me when I was younger?"

For these reasons, it's imperative that you really understand and comprehend the possibilities.

Now that you've read the book, you might have questions. Can I do this? Where do I begin?

Yes, you can build a financial future. Doing so involves beginning a journey of learning. There are possibilities and benefits to weigh. The subject of money is layered with nuance. I learn something new and exciting nearly every day. By reading this book, you've taken the first step on your own journey.

Knowing where you want to go is part of the formula. You need to set goals. But you also need to know where you are right now. Suppose you wanted to travel to Chicago. Would you go west? East? *Your direction depends on your starting point.*

So, ask yourself: Where am I now? What have I done so far? Answering those questions involves gathering some information:

- Family status—spouse? Do you have children? If so, how old are they?
- Current position—what is your current job and income?
- Goals—what are your retirement aspirations?
- Savings and Taxable Investments—what stocks, mutual funds and savings accounts do you have?
- Qualified retirement accounts—do you currently have a 401K or IRA?

- Defined benefit plans—are you vested in an employer-defined retirement plan?
- Real Estate—do you own property?
- Risk protection—health insurance? Auto? Property? Long-term disability? Term life insurance?
- Expenses—what mortgages, loans, and credit card debt are you carrying?
- Future expenses or income—Are college expenses in your future? Weddings? Inheritances? Are you vested in any company retirement plans?

Then, do your homework. Take an *objective* look at your options. If you happen to want more information from me, you are welcome to call for an appointment or e-mail me. I would be honored to help you with your personalized plan.

Contact Information:

David Saucer
Managing Director of Southern Region
*Strategy. Opportunity. Integration.*

Direct Line – 225.907.6000
Fax – 225.590.5596

www.CALLC.US
David.Saucer@CALLC.US

David A. Saucer

Baton Rouge | Little Rock
Los Angeles | Monroe | Nashville

# Appendix C: Suggested Reading

Now that you've begun your learning journey, here is some suggested reading to help you on your way:

- Becoming Your Own Banker (Nelson Nash)
- The Fall of Logic (Chase Chandler)
- Financial Independence in the 21$^{st}$ Century (Dwayne Burnell, MBA)
- The Great Wall Street Retirement Scam (Rick Bueter)
- How Privatized Banking Really Works (L. Carlos Lara and Robert P. Murphy, Ph.D.)
- The Millionaire Next Door (Thomas Stanley and William Danko)
- The Wealthy Physician (Chase Chandler)
- Opportunity Cost in Finance and Accounting (H. G. Heymann and Robert Bloom)
- The Richest Man in Babylon (George S. Clayson)
- The Trillion Dollar Meltdown (Charles R. Morris)
- The Wealthy Family (Chase Chandler)
- Understanding the Modern Culture Wars (Paul A. Cleveland, Ph.D.)

David A. Saucer

David A. Saucer

# Citations

"Brainy Quote" n.d. Web 22 Sep 2014.
http://www.brainyquote.com/

"Doubling Pennies" n.d. Web 22 Sep 2014.
http://mathforum.org/dr.math/faq/faq.doublin
g.pennies.html

"FDIC: Institution Directory." *FDIC: Institution Directory*. N.p., n.d. Web. 31 Dec. 2013

"Five Reasons 8 Out of 10 Businesses Fail."
Forbes. Forbes Magazine, n.d. Web. 27 July 2015.

"RMS Manual of Examination Policies." *Federal Deposit Insurance Corporation*, n.d. Web. 2
    Jan. 2014.
<http://www.fdic.gov/regulations/safety/manu
al/section3-7.pdf>.

"The Greatest Retirement Crisis in American
History." *Forbes*. Forbes Magazine. n.d. Web 26
June 2015.

"Things People Said: Bad Predictions" n.d. Web
22 Sep 2014.
http://www.rinkworks.com/said/predictions.sht
ml

"Welcome to InflationData.Com." Welcome to InflationData.com. N.p., n.d. Web. 05 Aug. 2015.

David A. Saucer

## About the Author

David is a lifelong resident of Louisiana. In the second year of seminary, he saw a girl in the lunch line and his life was changed—he's been happily married for more than 25 years.

David has two children. Kaleb is 23 and Chloe' is 21. His children are his greatest joy, and he proudly proclaims his greatest calling is to be a Dad.

As a licensed minister, he has joyfully served in many capacities. Over two decades, he has been involved in the financial services industry, helping thousands of families and business strategically plan for the future.

David's passion is family and making lasting memories.

# The CA$H Residence